Wilderness Cries:

Poems from the Heart of a Country Preacher

By Pastor Mike Vetsch

Wilderness Cries: Poems from the Heart of a Country Preacher
by Pastor Mike Vetsch

Printed in the United States of America

ISBN 9781624199622

www.xulonpress.com

A.V. was an older man whom I often visited at home. He had been married twice, and both wives were gone. His children were busy with their own lives and he could see out his window that life was going on without him. He often cried about this. Not so much about the pain, as about the boredom and monotony. He died a few years ago. This was written after one of our visits.

3-14-1999
He sits in his apartment,
Crying the tears
Of lonely old men.
Who wonder if life
Will visit them again.
Not just in dreams,
Or outside their windows,
But in their souls.
In their bellies.
Will they feel
The same fears?
Will they touch
Love's tears?
Will they be pierced
By sorrow's long spears?
I do not know.
Nor do they.
So they sit
Quietly,
Looking out onto a world
That ignores their tears.

W.S. was the first person I visited in the hospital. She said that she looked at the door, and kept looking up and up and up. (I am 6' 6") Over the years she has become a combination grandmother, girlfriend, and confidant. She survived two brain tumors, and still plays the piano at the nursing home. Her husband died a few years ago, and the last song we heard as we went out the door was <u>Go Rest High On That Mountain</u>. This was written that day.

2-11-1998
The sad notes
Lay their crescendos
Down.
Bringing a frown
And tears to my face.
To all in this place
As we say goodbye
To a good man.
The music haunts us.
Lingering in our hearts,
Long after the instruments
Lie still.
Perhaps it is because
We will never touch,
Never embrace,
Never see him chase
His grandchildren.
Perhaps it is because
We recognize
Our own fate.
But perhaps it is because
The song is too
Appropriate.

In elections, as in wars, everyone claims God is on their side. And they are right. God is on everyone's side. God loves everyone, and wants them to repent, and be forgiven, and live lives of joy, and peace, and faith. But we don't. Instead we make our claims on God, while God cries. This is from seeing what we do.

1-31-1996
God is
A socialist
Who clamors for us to work.
To share.

God is
A fundamentalist
Who demands our strict obedience
To his will.

God is
An artist
Who spends her day
Loving her craft.

God is
A wise old widow
Who has lived in pain so long,
She knows it can never
Be stopped.

God is
A nugget of gold,
Buried miles beneath the soil.
Waiting
For someone whose patience
Will discover it.

God is.

A.B. was a 2 year old who was diagnosed with Leukemia after some strange bruising and bleeding. She was a beautiful child who loved to sit in her dad's lap and watch the Green Bay Packers. She knew all the prayers in her prayer book. She loved to sing Jesus Loves Me. She loved her sisters and her cousins. She laughed with her grandmas. She knew pain. She even swore once. Something she picked up from her dad. She died in the autumn, and the darkness seemed too appropriate. These are from then.

10-21-2001
No one knows how long
We will sing our favorite song.
It may be Jesus Loves Me,
Or possibly,
Let It Be.
We do not know
How long we go.
But,
We have now.
Moments to live.
Time to give.
Now,
To share and dare.
To express our care.
And listen,
As others speak their words
To us.

10-21-2001

Darkness sits atop their home.
As if they each were alone
Together.
Grief fills the spaces in between.
A lingering darkness
That can't be seen,
But is felt
As the tears trickle down,
Until their eyes hurt,
And their souls feel empty,
And the dark night seems so bright
Compared to their hearts.

My wife and I like to go on bike trips. We wanted to circle Lake Superior, but with my schedule we had to break it up over 4 years. The first year was from Nipigon, Canada to Duluth, Minnesota. This was written after we returned home.

6-6-2002

We rode along the northern shore,

With wind,

And sun,

And so much more

Battering our souls,

And sore,

We rode together,

Until love

Began to pour

Like rain.

Every once in a while I find three words from a source, and write a poem using them. Usually that source is people. But one day I was at a volleyball camp, and no one was in the gym. I spun myself around, pointed, and walked that direction and used the first word I saw. I did that three times, and ended up with the words "smoking", "place", and "Midwest." This is the result.

7-10-1999
The embers were still warm
And the fireplace was still smoking,
Three hours after she left my place.
All that time spent
Racing over the Midwest
To find her.
To move her
Into loving me.
All those years.
All those tears.
All those fears
Shared,
Are now as meaningless
As the smoke that drifts up
Through the chimney.

J.W. was a young child whose best friend was diagnosed with cancer. They weren't sure if she was going to make it. When her mother asked that I put her friend on our prayer chain, I quickly agreed. No one should have to endure those times, but we do, too often. I wanted to write something for her. Something that could express the hope we have, even then. This is what came out.

2-25-1998

You are too young to hear

Or know

Of death.

You must first

Taste life,

As it runs unfettered

Down gorges.

Into streams.

Until it seems

That there is no end.

But you will know,

As your life long friend

Lies dying,

And all the crying in the world

Is useless.

Because no matter how hard we try,

How much we care,

Sometimes,

5 years is a lifetime.

The T's. are a typical farm family. They have the same joys, quarrels, and issues that everyone else has. When the patriarch was dying, the entire family gathered at the hospital to hold vigil. They communicated as well, and as poorly, as everyone does during these times. It got to be longer than expected, and as anyone who has endured this knows, with every breath there is hope, and there is anguish. This is from that experience.

1-16-1998
They play their cards.
They play as bards.
Reminiscing
On the old days.
And they touch their grandpa,
To tell him
They love him.

They say their prayers.
They voice their cares.
Hoping beyond hope,
For another moment.
And when grandpa asks,
They tell him,
They love him.

For sixteen days
This goes on.
Until he gasps out,
And nothing returns.
A few days later
They gather mid-morning,
In mourning,
And they bury him
Deep in the soil.

continued

All the while,
In their way,
In their hearts,
They tell him,
They love him.

P.H. was an energetic, warm woman who hugged everyone. She had survived five brain tumors, and lived life on her terms, and we all understood that and embraced it. The last time her tumor shrunk she told me she knew why, even though the doctors were baffled. She said it was our church. I agreed, telling her everyone associated with our church had things in their brain shrink too. She laughed, as did the congregation when I told them this story. During one of the times I thought she would not last more than a few days, this was written. I thought I would speak it at her funeral, when that day comes.

11-25-2003
Let us take this day to cry.
To remember she
Who had to die.
To let our hearts shudder,
And our souls sigh,
As we say
Our last goodbye.
And let us sit tonight
In deepest dark.
To face directly
The stark reality
Of life without her.
Let us cry our tears
As the sun sets west,
But then,
Let us wake,
And remember her best
The way she lived.
Full of life.
Full of love.
Full of faith and joy.
Sharing herself
As if she were a toy.

continued

And though now she spins
In distant galaxies,
She will always be
In our hearts,
And in our memories.

After my divorce, I was often tired, lonely, and busy. Not only with work, but with the things I did for fun and to pass the time. But sometimes it would catch up with me. At those times, when my mind and heart were fatigued, words would come. This is from one of those times.

5-22-1997
I cry to God for relief.
Release.
For peace.
But I only hear the wind rustle the pines
Outside my door.
Is God alive anymore?
Does he not know my pain?
My woe?
And so, I return to my child's room
To hear his breathing
As he sleeps
Nestled in his blanket.
I return to my wife,
As she cuddles a pillow,
Oblivious,
To my meanderings.
I return and remember
That when I have cried with her,
She did not give any answers,
But she cried with me.
And when I loved her most deeply
She did not cheaply tease or hurt,
But she held me in silence.
And so I began to believe,
To conceive,
That God's silence is not anger or apathy,
But wisdom.

continued

Grace.
That were God to show his face,
It would be tear stained.
Ingrained
With thousands of years of pain.
God is not silent
From apathy or anger,
But God shares our silences,
Like two lovers lying together,
With smiles on their faces.

There was a week where I did two funerals. One was for an elderly man who dropped dead in his bathroom, and was found by his wife. The other was a young man who drowned. As we grieved these two deaths, it made me wonder the philosophical question which only someone who had not personally endured them could ask, which one was more painful. This is from that time.

6-21-1995
Which is more difficult,
To grieve the loss of a seventeen year old,
The loss of potential love,
Or to grieve your husband's loss
After 59 years together?
To miss the history
And the future
Of your love together?

This is like asking,
Which is more difficult,
To climb Mount Everest,
Naked and alone,
Or to swim an ocean?

Some days are like tangible hope. As if light and life can be touched, and moved, and played with. As if God gives us these things as toys, and we can share them with each other, and hold on to them for those darker days. This came from a time like that.

7-1-1999
The moon and her cohorts
Have all night to play.
So they dance and sing
Until the break of day.
Until the sun rises
And showers her surprises
On the rest of us.
And then the moon and her friends
Put an end
To their revelry,
And sleep.
Until it is time again
To dance.

As a pastor, sometimes I think about funerals and weddings long before they occur. I have a file in my office where I keep stories about people that I might use at their funerals. And sometimes my imagination thinks about things that might happen to people. Sometimes those like me. Sometimes those much different. These are examples of what happens when the imagination plays.

12-12-1997
Let the sun and moon
Disappear.
Let the long night
Begin.
No hope for dawn.
All hope is gone
With you.
Let the tears begin
Their endless flow,
Because I know no way
To stop them.
Let my heart too,
Be stilled,
As yours is.
Let my heart be stilled
And sit nestled beneath the earth,
Next to yours,
Because that is where
They belong.

6-15-2000
Long will I remember
That morning in November
When peace
Came to an end.
When I took a bend
too fast,
And put an end to our past,
And our future.
All I know about that moment
Is the pain,
And the rain that fell down
Upon her auburn curls.
Where blood,
And raindrops,
And my tears swirled
Around a crooked smile.
I can never forget
The sorrow that consumed me.
And the darkness that lingers
Still.

L.H. was the first custodian I had as a pastor. And he was an angel. He arrived an hour before I did, and did all the work. He poured communion wine. He rang the church bells. He turned on all the lights. And during the week he cleaned and was there for any and every event. He was even the cemetery custodian. He knew where almost everyone was buried. And now, appropriately, he is there. This was written several months after his death.

10-27-1996

There comes a time,
Every Sunday,
When I sit in my chair
And wait for him
To peek around the corner.
With his sly smile,
And jokes,
And warmth.
But (I hate buts)
There is no more
Warmth
In his body
As it lays
Less than a hundred feet
From where my feet
Sit propped up.
And so,
Every Sunday,
I sit.
I wait.
I remember.
I wonder.

Even before I was a pastor, I was involved in Christmas programs, as a kid, youth director and intern. What struck me one day, is how close they are to what probably really happened. Everyone has their plans for how they are going to go, and it never works that way. The problems and mistakes come, and people overlook them, and love conquers. Sounds like what Christmas is all about. This was written for a newsletter article.

11-20-1996
The angels sang
In their bright array,
"Glory to God."
"Peace on earth."
"Halleluiah
To the Savior's birth."
Or so the tradition goes.
But I think reality
Was a little different.
Like our Christmas pageants,
With the child crying in the third row,
The angel's wings falling off,
The third king kicking his camel,
Joseph and Mary not saying their lines,
And the beaming,
proud faces
of parents.
The real love
For these imperfect children.
That is Christmas,
Or so
The tradition goes.

Long before I decided to go on sabbatical and think about the church as a place in the wilderness, I knew that it was an important theme. From the Hebrew people, to Jesus, to us, the wilderness has been an important part of what we all go through in our lives. Sometimes it is intentional. Sometimes it is what we must endure.

2-13-1997

Jesus had one.

As soon as he was baptized,

He ended up

With a wilderness experience.

The Hebrew people had one.

To be free from slavery,

They wandered in theirs

For forty years.

We all have them.

Times of living in wastelands

Wondering

If it will turn out OK,

If it is worth going on,

If anybody cares.

And the funny thing is,

If you are patient,

Long suffering,

Faithful,

You end up

In a land of milk,

And honey,

And resurrection.

One of the things we see as pastors is the suffering that people endure. Because of the sinful world we live in, we all endure it. And pastors see much of it. People come to us in grief. We visit them in their most vulnerable moments. And even we suffer. This was written as I pondered the suffering of a child in the hospital.

3-22-1997
Tears come again
For a child,
Whose bald head sweats
From his simple act
Of opening a door.
Tears come again
For a father,
Who tries to put a cap on his child
As he runs off to play.
Tears come,
For all children of God
Who live in their suffering.

One of the things pastors deal with is relationships. We deal with them when they don't work. We try to cultivate them as we minister to people. We know how important they are.

4-9-1997
A laugh
Shared by an old couple
Over an inside joke
That took 60 years
To create.

A tickle
Of two minds
Too fickle
For others to find.

How do you explain
Or understand
The intricacies
Of relationships?
Of you and I,
And they and we,
And he and she?

I do not believe
We should even try
To figure them out,
But
Live them out.
In the joys,
The tears,
The moments,
That cover
The years.

Sometimes relationships and their adventures are what carry us through life. We share memories, embraces, tears, and a host of other poignant moments. This was written to remind myself of that truth.

5-3-1997
Love
Does not consist
Of insistencies,
But of embraces,
Laughter,
Guffaws,
Faux paus,
And silly little notes.
Antidotes
To the pains
Of a sinful,
Broken,
World.

One of the things I believe was good about the Reformation was the translation of the Bible into common language. It allowed people to read it and see what it says. The problem is that people will disagree about what it means. The solution is simple. Talk. I wrote this years ago, but as I was going through my poems to decide which to include, I realized that this was still true, and still important.

5-3-1997
Roots go deeper
When there's a drought.
Faith grows stronger
After doubt.
Seeds scatter,
But never far
From the stalk.
Hearts move,
And sway,
But never beyond
Talk.

Sometimes people get angry at God. I don't mind that. To be in a real relationship, we need to express everything, including joy, anger and sorrow. And that includes our relationship with God.

5-25-1997

How can you release

The tears that come?

Where is the peace

Available to some?

How can you

Let go of the rage,

When God is the object

Of your spite?

How can you vent?

Grieve?

Continue to believe

That it is all right

To even go on?

I don't know how.

I just know

That we do

And

That it hurts.

There is a large cemetery that sits beside the church I pastor. Actually, there are even three graves under the office. They were left when the addition was built in the 1920s. I often think about the many people buried there, and the grief and sorrow, and even joy that has been felt as people stood burying their loved ones. Sometimes I think about what others have felt. This is from one of those meanderings.

6-21-1997
Raindrops fall
In large somber tears
From the trees
Where we played
Among the gravestones.
Gray clouds
Pass over the bluff.
Toward the picket fence.
The house.
The dense colors,
Sounds,
Smells
Of the gathering
Are forgotten
By the numbness
Of this visit.
All is lost
In the haze
Of memory,
Save,
For those tear drops
That fall
So sullen.

After dealing with a lot of funerals, I have wondered what it would be like to lose someone as close as a spouse or child. It has not happened yet, but may. Sometimes when I think about it, I write down what I think I might feel. I have no idea if I will feel what I have written, but this is what came.

6-2-1997
I slip my hand into hers,
Like we have done
For the past 43 years.
Only now it is cold,
Except for the warm tear
I drop on it.
How do you go on,
When every step
Is alone?
How do you live,
When the children are old and grown,
And the house creaks from the wind,
And you hear her voice,
And the tears come rushing,
And your stomach hurts,
And you must sit down?
How do you live?

Before I was a pastor, I realized how hard it was to say goodbye. For several summers I worked at Bible Camp and there were lots of goodbyes to lots of good people. And it was hard. One day on the way home, I had to stop the car and simply cry, because I might never see most of these people again. As a pastor, we also have many goodbyes. And they never get any easier. These are from a day where I remembered how hard they can be.

8-14-1997
Every time I say goodbye
A tear wells up
Deep inside.
A sigh comes.
Because there is nothing
I can do
Except hurt
And hope.
That is the price
Of love.

8-14-1997
A hug.
A tear.
A goodbye.
A fear
That this may be the last.
That this becomes a past,
Dim memory.
How do we hold on
To the times that matter?
How do we cling
To the loves that shatter
Our concepts?
How do we clutch
Those strings
That connect us,
That make our hearts sing
With the harmonies
We've never heard before?

We just hold on
A little tighter,
A little longer.
Until finally,
We're stronger
And we can share the tears
Of goodbye.

Following my divorce, I didn't write much about how I felt. Between being busy with work, and just wanting to not think so much about it, I just pushed it aside until later. And it came. These are among the first poems I wrote about the pain and sadness that came.

12-12-1997
When
Will I again
Touch willing breast
To breast?
Who will watch
As I lay
Crying on the floor
Now?
From whose hands
Will the fingers come
To massage my cares
Away?
And who will share
Tears
To mingle in our bed
As we lay our heads
Close?

12-12-1997
Once again
My love is left up to my imagination.
Once again
Sitting up in the early morning
Writing.
Hoping.
Dreaming
Of a new
Her.
Once again
Pain,
Loneliness,
Boredom,
And being busy
Pass my slow days.
Once again
My laundry
Receives more attention
Than my heart.
Once again
Isolation
Is the machination
For how I work.
Once again
A hearts needs its armor.
Once again
The tears fall slowly.
Singly.
Alone.
Once again
The bed holds one.
Once again.

Being a pastor is an interesting career. There are people to counsel, administrative tasks, sermons to prepare, and countless other things. But it often seems our primary task is to battle sin and its consequences. This was written when I considered what I did.

1-6-1998
I bear the secrets
Of a community
Nestled within the hills.
Virile young men
Trying to impose their will
On virile,
But insecure,
Women
Old widows,
Who haggle over gossip
Like it was fish in a market.
As a minister,
I fight the sinister
Within us all.

One of the popular movements that happened during my early ministry was the church growth movement. Personally, I didn't think too much about it. I was in an older, rural congregation where people were dying and moving out. We were probably not going to grow. I was also bothered by the idea of numbers, which some people put too much emphasis on. So, I wrote this.

2-10-1998
What does it mean
To be touched
By God?
To be a people who gather
As church?
Who seem to lurch
Left,
Right,
Sideways?
How can you tell
If you grow
Or not?
Is growth measured
With each member
Or within each member?
How do you measure
Love?
Faith?
Relationship?
You don't.
You don't waste time measuring.
You make time
To be.

One of the things I do every month is visit the local nursing homes, although they aren't very local. Some are 50 miles away. But it is important to do. We usually have around a dozen people, and visits keep them connected with the congregation. It can be the only time they get to share their spirituality. This was written after one particular visit with a member.

2-18-1998
We made beautiful music
Together.
Our hands touching
So slightly.
So tenderly.
My face
Inches from her ear.
Neither of us
Cared about the world
Outside that room
Because
We made music
Together.
Her lips moved
And so did mine
In unison.
We made beautiful music
Together
As we spoke
The Lord's Prayer.
I almost cried
When I left her bedside,
But I told her,
"God bless you,
I will come again,"
And she
Thanked me.

I was walking down the driveway to get the mail one day, and there was a rose petal on the ground. As I imagined the loneliness of that rose petal, I remembered that sometimes this can be our loneliness. We fail, we fall, and we wonder, "Are we loved? " This poem was my answer.

3-13-1998
A rose petal drops
Slowly to the ground.
The wind makes it flutter.
But it still falls.
Only to lie
Forgotten.
No one will stop to smell it.
No one will ever tell it
"What a lovely flower."
No,
One will.
The one who created it.
Created us.
Created all.
That one will watch.
Remember.
Love.
That one
Will stoop down
Like he has
Before.

A.L. was a business man, an entrepreneur, really. And from his many ventures, he had gained a wisdom that helped him when he was diagnosed with cancer. It taught him how to die a good death. Not one where you want to be alone, away from friends and family, but where you want to tell those you love the words that need to be told. And A. did this. He died a good death.

4-6-1998
You died a good death.
Able to talk,
To share memories,
And create new ones.
To feel a touch upon your brow
And live in your now.
You died a good death.
A loving wife by your side.
Her tears on your face,
And an embrace,
As she deeply cried
For your loss.
You died
A good death.
Able to say
What needed to be said
Before this world
Saw you dead
And buried.
You
Died
A good death.

God does not always follow our plans. Sometimes it is because our plans are wrong. Sometimes it is because God tests us. Sometimes we just won't know why. But God does what God will do, and we follow accordingly.

6-12-1998
The music
Which God marches to
Is not a Sousa march
Or an eloquent symphony.
No,
God marches without syncopation.
A stop here,
To help the widow cry her tears.
A side trip there,
To give words of impact
That will last for years.
God does not march at all,
According to our definition.
It is more like
A leisurely stroll by a gardener
As she examines
Her roses.

Pastors spend a lot of time in hospitals. We sit in waiting rooms. We visit in intensive care units. We give communion, and pray, and talk. This was written with many of these visits in mind.

6-23-1998
Tubes criss and cross,
Getting in the way
As I try to feed her.
Nurses hover too close.
Hearing us,
As we try to whisper intimacies.
Doctors and chaplains
Come in and out.
And she still suffers.
She still dies.
But all is not lost.
I may never see her again,
But she gave me a lesson
I will never forget.
We must all live
Each moment.
She taught me,
That not only must we
Not be afraid to die,
We must not be
Afraid to live.

One day while visiting a parishioner at a nursing home, I saw a woman in a wheel chair just sitting by the window. It appeared she was sleeping, and no one ever checked her to see if she was alive or not. It influenced me so much, that when I got home, I wrote the following.

8-25-1998
A flick of the right index finger
Is all he can accomplish
Now.
Dim memories
Flow in and out
Of his fractured mind.
The synapses weary
From the same ancestral path.
He sits in the wheelchair
In front of the bay window,
Warmed by the sun.
He has outlived his youth.
His friends.
His life.
But he still lingers.
His wish is to go on.
His desire is to join
Those many others.
But he has no say.
And so he sits,
Every day,
Numb to pain.
Numb to life.

Sometimes pastors need to pull back emotionally, so we can survive. To care for people takes a lot of energy and strength. And it can't be done without a respite. This was written when I needed some time to relax.

11-6-1998
If you feel my heart receding,
It is only to prevent it
From bleeding
Profusely.
Like an oak tree,
Whose leaves wither and fall,
Whose inner sap
Lets it survive,
I pull back.
Pull in.
So I too
May survive
The long,
Cold,
Winter.

One of the epiphanies I have gotten is that we are to live our lives as the created people we are. Not better. Not worse. But as what we are. It is part of faith. To trust that God created us, and that despite our sinfulness, we are still loved. I discovered it once as I lay in a hospital with Rheumatic Fever. I also remember it once in a while. God loves us, so we may live out who we are, with integrity. We express our emotions. We apologize for our mistakes. We live our lives as a response to grace. This was written one night as I pondered this truth.

11-7-1998
Why do you hold back
What you feel?
What are you saving it for?
In forty years,
Give or take,
I will have to forsake
My life.
Until then,
I plan to live
All my life.
From the dross
And beyond.
To feel every loss
And every gain.
I plan to live,
Despite what the world may say.
Because I have lain,
Bound,
In a hospital bed.
I have been fed
The lie of security.
Whose chains fall away
Only when we die,
Or when we live.

One of the things poets and pastors write about and speak about is love. From the passions of lust, to the self sacrifice of parental love, to God's grace, people have wanted to know about this wonderful, crazy thing we share. This is one of many poems about love. One of the ones I like.

11-11-1998
Love is a garden
With weeds to be pulled,
Roses to be culled,
A winter
To be lulled into boredom
While you wait.

Love is an ember.
Begun from a spark
Years ago.
Barely able to remember,
Because time,
Memories,
Life,
Have passed.

Love is a promise.
Unspoken,
Unbroken,
Between two souls
Who mingle themselves
Until you can't tell one
From the other.

Love is a song
To be danced to,
Or hummed along.

continued

49

Spreading joy for a moment or two,
Until the refrain is over
And you join the silence
Of knowing
That love is.

H.H. was a 100 year old woman with an incredibly sharp mind. She had been a teacher for over 50 years, and didn't marry until she was in her later years. A few years before her death, she taught me the Norwegian Table Prayer so I could use it at our Lutefisk dinner. She was a teacher to the end. This was written after one of our visits.

11-29-1998

A century alive

And still able to teach

Love

As she did

Most of her life.

Teaching

With her words,

With her wisdom

That love,

And touch,

And looking into each other's eyes

And caring,

Are what life is all about.

Her smile,

A century old,

Still churns with the joy

Her childhood recollections

Stir.

And her eyes,

Embodied wisdom,

Make you want to dance,

As her affections

Trickle in

To your own soul.

One day, while I was looking out the window of the parsonage, there was a single leaf left on a tree. It fit what I was feeling, so I wrote this.

12-18-1998
All the leaves have fallen,
Except for one.
What makes her
Remain?
Was she not battered enough
By the winds?
Did not the cold rescind
Her will?
Why does she still
Remain?
I can not answer.
But I am glad.
Because that lone,
Stubborn leaf,
Gives me hope.
If she can stay
For just one more day,
If she chooses to remain,
Despite the pain,
Well,
Maybe I can too.

All the leaves have fallen
Except for one.

If you are human, you will endure suffering. There is no escaping it. Every one of us has to go through it. There are losses of friends, jobs, health, family, and more. If you live, you will suffer. This was written one day when I was tired.

12-26-1998
I have lived
Far more than my years should know.
Far more than my tears would show.
I have tasted sorrow
As it fell down upon me
Like a spring filled creek
Engorging the river
And rising up the banks.
I have lost
Friends
Who had been an intimate
Part of my life.
I have lived
With holes in my heart
That may scab over,
But never
Can be filled,
Because the one who was there
Is gone.
Never
To be replaced.
This has happened
Because
I
Have lived.

One of the things pastors deal with is regrets. People regret what they have done. They regret what has been done to them. They often regret meeting with pastors as it can bring guilt and shame. But regrets can be futile. There is no turning back. You can only go on, and hopefully, change.

2-14-1999
Life is not a book
Where pages turn
And you can look back.
There is no editing to be done,
Except,
In the moment.
All the red pens in the world
Won't do you any good
When you ask for forgiveness,
Promise to never say it again,
And swear it was a mistake.
Life grants no erasures,
Save for death.

Sometimes it feels as if we are alone in the battle against sin and evil. As if our voice is the only one that cries out against injustice. And sometimes this is true. So, we have to be the ones who shout, until we can shout no more.

2-18-1999

I have

But my voice

To shout down the monsters

That oppress the world.

To scream out against

All the injustice I see

But can do little about.

I am one.

Not strong enough to change tyranny.

I have my voice

Only.

But I will use it

Until it becomes a whisper

And a memory.

I do not remember who this was written for, if it was written for anyone in particular. But as I looked back, it was appropriate for many people I have been involved with.

3-1-1999
Her ardent prayers
To all those soothsayers
Did not save her.
She still died.
I still cried
As I stood by her side
Hoping.
But now I realize
That in one sense
Her prayers were answered.
She is finished
With pain
Now.
She is off,
Beyond this world,
In some distant,
verdant pasture
Looking directly
Into the face
Of God.

I was the only one in the room when I.H. died. I was there for a while, holding vigil. He was an old man who had been in the nursing home for a time. I was looking at his bulletin board, and noticed how little there was. As I pondered what I would be saying about him at his funeral, I realized that sometimes there isn't much.

3-6-1999
Tattered papers
And old Christmas cards
Pinned to a bulletin board
Are not much
To remember a man by
When he's gone.
When labored breaths cease.
When we believe
He is at peace.
What do we erect
As a monument
To a life of care?
A life of toil?
A life of tilling the dirt,
Loving his soil?
We do not erect
Anything.
We just keep planting.
Nourishing.
Harvesting,
Like we have before.

The call of a pastor is not only to care for their parishioners and the congregation they serve, but also to serve the larger church. One of the tasks for that is to develop leaders, to pass the faith on to the next generations, so that they will become faithful disciples. It is about making sure good church leadership will continue. This was written with that in mind.

3-10-1999
Planted in the ground,
Unable to move anywhere,
Except up and out
As its nature calls.
So she shoots forth
From little green shoot
To large cedar.
She grows for years.
Giving shade,
Branches for nests,
And leaves that fall,
Decay,
And nourish the soil.
And then one day,
She falls over
Dead.
Her trunk slowly eaten by insects,
Until a new seed sprouts
From the rich nutrients
And life
Goes on.

At the congregation I serve, we average about a hundred people at our worship services. But it's an interesting number, because there are many who miss services, and there are still about a hundred or so. I was thinking about this, and also the normal angst of whether what I preach is getting through to people, and this is what came.

5-20-1999

Maybe that was the day
The preacher had you in mind,
But you missed it
Because you couldn't find the right shoes.
Maybe this was the time
Your enemy swore
To offer forgiveness
Forever more,
But you were not there
Because you hadn't washed your hair.
Or maybe
You came.
You saw.
You felt a whisper in your soul
As you looked around
And saw many
Who should never be forgiven,
But are.

One of the things I often do is to ask for three words from someone, and then write a poem using those words. The following poem was done at Bible Camp, but what made it special for me is that a young couple, whose wedding I was doing, saw it, and they surprised me by using it in their wedding. That was special.

6-27-1999 Doc
"Chartreuse, stem, string"
A chartreuse rose
Does not begin
With the stem.
There is seed,
Soil,
Water,
And toil,
All coming together
To produce
This beautiful gift.
It is a lot like relationships.
This invisible string,
From my heart to yours,
Is not some miracle.
It is the accumulation
Of all our talk,
All our touch,
All our tears,
And other such poignant moments,
Until we too
Become a beautiful gift
To each other.

Pastors often move from joy to sorrow and back, sometimes very quickly. We might make a hospital visit to see a newborn, and find out that one of our parishioners is there after an accident or heart attack. That is part of the job. But I think it can happen to everyone, because life can be so funny and fickle.

6-5-1999
How can you move
From the birth of a child
To the death of her grandmother
So easily?
Like a train that clicks and clacks
Through sleepy Midwest towns,
No one knows
What goes on inside.
How can you feel
The tears that swell
Just behind your eyes
As you hold your hands
And say your prayers,
And then,
In an instant,
Feel as if there are no cares,
And smile?
How can you do these things,
And stay sane?
How can you not,
If you live?

As I have ministered for the past 19 years, some poems have come from looking at life in general. Not just those in this congregation or community, but the world. These are from doing that.

7-6-1999
When your sorrows have assailed you
And grief seems to have impaled you,
What do you do?
Do you anticipate the stages,
From denial to grave rages?
Do you try to scream it out,
Or try to hide and pout?
Or are you just like the rest of us
And struggle
Just to breathe.

8-9-1999
If you live,
You will lie.
You will cry.
You will die.
There is no escape.
We can not deny
What will happen.
We can only embrace it.
We can not chase it away
With imaginary kingdoms
Or fancy schemes.
We can only accept it.
Accept ourselves
And live out God's hope and dream
Of people,
Honest,
Open people
Loving one another.

8-9-1999
In my church
The same hands that wash the dishes
Tenderly caress grandchildren.
The same lips
That swear at referees
Thank God for a child who can run.
The same legs
That waitress 12 hours a day
Slowly walk to an altar rail
On Communion Sundays.
The same ears
That hear complaints at the garage
Listen attentively
as the Order for Confession
And Forgiveness
draws to a close.
The same eyes
That see problems in others
See problems in themselves.
And the same hearts
That love me,
Love God.
Love Jesus.
Love others.

The first poem I wrote as a pastor was inspired by the setting. The congregation is in a valley, surrounded by hills and farms. It is called Church Valley, and the peace you feel is almost tangible. This was my first response to being there.

10-23-1993
A breeze blows gently
Over dry brown stalks.
A cowbell rings
In the valley next.
God pulls the covers dark
Over another day.
And we sleep,
Cradled in his hand.

Sometimes we ask questions that are not easy to answer. They may be theological. They may be from suffering. They may be from both, like the following.

7-7-1994
What does it mean
That Judas
Was given the bread and wine?
What does it mean
That children suffer
Too many times?
What does it mean?

My grandmother died the first year I was a pastor. She was a woman of deep faith and had been thrilled that I went to seminary and became a pastor. My grief came in spurts, which made me realize that it often happens that way, especially for pastors who are involved in so much. During one of those times I was struggling, and had the time, these words came.

11-29-1993
My grandmother died
The other day.
And I took a few moments
To mourn,
In between writing a sermon,
Teaching a class,
Baptizing an infant,
Meeting an alcoholic,
Typing the newsletter,
Repairing a speaker,
And sleeping.

And I wonder why
There's a clergy shortage?

One of the things that happens when you minister to people is you imagine how people think. You wonder about what your parishioners are thinking when they go through the sorrows and joys of life. You think about what other people feel as they live their lives. Sometimes you wonder about people who have no faith. And whether what you think is what they think or not, it doesn't matter. What matters is that you think about them. This is from some imagining about a certain kind of people.

12-18-1993
Another Christmas
Alone.
Had I the money
I would buy a gun
And deliver myself.
Alcohol
Takes too long.
There are memories
Of her
Before it happened.
But they are too old,
As I am.
Ready to wither.
Like a plant
Unwatered.
Yet the rains come.
Just barely enough
For one small leaf
To remain.

As fun as youth gatherings can be, they can also be hard. Having been to countless gatherings, and conventions, and camp outings, I sometimes weary of all the energy and noise that are there. Sometimes I would rather be home, with family, and share some simple conversation and laughter. I don't think I am the only one. This was written when I was away and missed my wife.

4-8-1994
Muted whispers through a door.
Sitting,
Wishing,
For a little more
Time
To spend with my beloved.

Career and caress
Come to push and shove.

Memories return
Of hallways shared.
Other youth.
Others who dared
Open a door.
Jump on a bed.
Laugh too loud.

Those memories
Of being together
Do not take away
The ache
Of being apart.

As a pastor, I see the destruction that can come from someone saying the wrong thing. And it doesn't take much, a wrong word, or a joke that didn't work. A secret blurted out. It doesn't take much to hurt people, and sometimes those words and that hate can last a life time. This is a reminder that small things have power.

4-26-1994
A little mosquito bites.
Leaving a mark
And malaria.

Who would have thought
Death could be so painful
From such a small,
Small thing?

A wrong word
Escapes
From my lips.
Who would have thought?

During my first Lenten season as a pastor, I had eight funerals. That doesn't seem so much now, but my first year, and with three in one week, and youthful enthusiasm foolishly planning and carrying out lock-ins and all the other activities, it was difficult. Sometimes it felt as if there was just a cloud over me. This is what came during that time.

5-3-1994
Piano sounds
From an overplayed tape.
Clock ticks.
No thoughts of escape.
Work,
Like a large cloud
That holds the sun behind,
Sits in my way.
Oh, I see brightness,
On the trees
Across the road.
I sense some warmth,
As a wind slowly moves by.
But that cloud sits,
Follows,
Moving as I move.
What a day this turned out to be.

Some moments in our lives are not best captured in words, but in vague grunts or gestures. I thought about this one day and decided someone's life could be captured in the following way.

6-22-1994
"Hah," she laughed,
As I squirted her
With water from a squirt gun.
Little memory
For a later time.

"Aah," they murmured,
As she walked down the aisle.
Only to release
My hand.

"Oooh," she moaned,
As her child came,
Crying
Into the world
Of bright light.

"Mmph," she sniffled,
As she watched
Her father buried.

"Hey," she shouted at the nurses
In the home.

"Ow," she cried.

The Bible study of our Bible camp in 1994 was about God as "I Am". As I thought about this, I also realized that we are when we do God's work.

7-8-1994
When I stroke the cheek
Of an old senile woman
In a nursing home,

When I share a goofy tale
Of cosmic flatulence
As smoke ascends
From a campfire,

When I laugh with a child
Who stumbled into the pool
And came up smiling,

When I speak the words,
"Ashes to ashes,"
Holding back tears,

When I,
Then I
Am.

In the summer of 1994 a friend and I took a canoe trip. It was a rugged trip. The weather was difficult. The lightning was so bad the first night that we hardly slept. We later admitted that we had both slept on our sides, trying to make it less likely to be struck. We pushed ourselves, ignoring fatigue and common sense at times. We went off the normal routes. My friend twisted his ankle. But we both agreed, it was a good trip. Not because of, or despite the difficulty, but because we did it.

7-10-1994
Another adventure gone.
A moment shared
Where we dared.

Do you think I speak
Of dragging a canoe upstream?
I don't.
I remember the adventure
Of sharing.
Of reaching deep into ourselves
And laughing.
And wondering.
And hoping.

I speak of the joys
Of physical fatigue.
Spiritual explosion.

I speak too much.
I should smile
Remember.
Enjoy.

As a pastor, I am often asked to speak. To say the prayers, give words of comfort, give blessings and benedictions. And sometimes they are hard to come by. It is something all pastors struggle with. Because they are often difficult times. Because they do not seem good enough. Because sometimes word are not enough. I do not remember the occasion for this particular poem, but it resonates often with me.

7-14-1994
How do you describe
The tears that swell unseen
Just behind your eyes?

How can you explain
The loss you feel
When confined to a wheelchair?

How do you capture
The laughter
For others to share?

How can you give meaning
To something
Beyond human comprehension?

What words or gestures
Are to be used
In those unspeakable moments?

In the summer of 1994 the national church had a youth gathering in Atlanta. As we were down there, experiencing things many of my rural youth had never seen, I imagined what it would be like to live there. Much of it is the same. Pain and sorrow. Joy and boredom. Work and worry. This is what came from my meanderings.

7-25-1994
I rode the MARTA
To my house.
Past people
I barley know,
Yet hold me in contempt,
Hate,
Apathy.

I walk down the stairs.
Humidity fatigues me.
And I smile
As I spot my roof.
Picking up my steps
As I travel
To my sanctuary.

When someone you love dies, you mourn. Even if you know they are in a better place. Even if you know you will see them again. Because when you lose someone, it's not about the future. It's about what you shared. This comes from that truth.

8-2-1994
All that time spent
Getting to know you.
To trust.
To feel.
All that time talking.
Being.

And then,
It is time
For goodbye.

How can we say it?
How can we mean it?

Our religious belief tells us,
Some day.
But my heart still cries.
Still longs
To sit by the pool
Laughing.
To sit on a bus,
Playing hearts.
To sit,
Watching,
As you grow.

Most pastors I know work very hard. There is a lot to do. Caring for hundreds of people, listening, consoling, chiding, teaching, preaching, loving, all take time and energy. And sometimes it takes its toll. But the funny thing is, after the breakdown, there is a moment of wakening. You remember why you do it. This is from one of those times.

8-19-1994
Fatigue overcomes me.
Succumbs me
Until I fall
Fast asleep.
Reading stopping.
Newspaper dropping.
Dreams come.
A moment of joy
Where I am loved.
Then sudden terror
As monsters jump out.

Awakening,
To a bright sun
Setting on the western bluff.
It is enough
To have driven those miles
Met smiles with smiles.
Loved,
Another week.

Early on I got the question that often comes. Where is God? Where is God in our pain? Where is God when tragedy strikes? Where is God when loved ones die, especially kids? This is an answer.

2-18-1995
Where is God
In my tears?

Where is God
As we break up
Again?

Where is God
As I place my child
In the ground?

Where is God
As I drive to work
Listening to an old disco song?

Where is God
As I march my daughter down an aisle,
Ever reluctant
To let go my grasp?

Where is God
As the sweat beads down my neck
In the hot summer heat?

Where is God?

Hanging on a cross,
With tears,

continued

77

Blood,
Sweat,
And agony.
Crying out
"Father, forgive them."

I include an original poem for every newsletter article I write. It is just something I have always done. For one Easter newsletter article I thought about what Easter really was for different people. This was that poem.

3-23-1995
Easter is here,
For the recent widow,
Who stands at the hospital window
Looking at her new grandchild.
Easter is here,
Come to the child
Who broke her leg
As her cast is cut off.
Easter is here,
In a check
Made out to a couple
About to lose their home.
Easter is here,
In a tomb
Containing a few bands of cloth.
Easter is here.

One of the most important, poignant and interesting things pastors do is administer Holy Communion. There is something special about seeing someone extend their hand for a tangible piece of grace.

4-13-1995
A common cup
Filled with wine
Held in my hand
As I stand facing the altar.

A small wafer.
Flat-tasting.
Sticky as it moistens
And holding to my tongue

Whispers in the congregation.
Feelings of obligation.
Oblation.
Celebration.
And then they come
To the upper room
To receive.
Holding out their hands.
Pleading for more.
How can I ignore?
How can I not smile
And give the gifts
Of body.
Blood.
Life.

Like anyone, pastors struggle when the day is nice and we are stuck inside with work that must be done. When there is a sermon to be written, a person on the phone, a letter to send, and programs to be planned, it is hard to focus when God gives you a day where he just wants you to go outside and play. This was written on one of those days.

5-11-1995
How can one work
When the sun beams
Call you out
As they blast through the windows?
God calls to play
Today.
A sermon awaits.
A homily to tell
Why we love.
Why we honor mothers,
Children,
Graduates.
But a better sermon
Sits outside
In the warmth
Of a sunny day.

There is something inside us that makes us cling to things, even when it is not healthy. There are people who stay with their abusers. Not healthy. There are addicts. Not healthy. There are many of us, pastor's included, who cling to beliefs, ideas, and thought patterns that just aren't necessary. This poem was written without realizing that was where it was headed. I had intended to write about what it meant to care about something delicate and gentle, but something inside me changed it. I don't know why.

6-2-1995
I hold an eggshell
As tenderly as I can.
But it drops.
It cracks.
It breaks,

Again and again.
I grasp it tighter,
But not too tight.
But again,
It drops.
I hold my precious eggshell
For years.
Gluing it.
Taping it.
Praying it will hold.
Until one day
I drop it again
And realize
I don't need
That stupid egg.

I have heard many fellow pastors say that when we do a lot of work for a sermon, and think it is good, people often don't compliment us. But when we don't have enough time, and feel ill prepared, that is when we get lots of compliments about how great that sermon was. This asks that question.

7-9-1995
Why is it,
That when I take credit,
Everything
Goes for naught?
But,
When I give credit to God,
Everything
Works for good?

Why is it
That the mornings
I expect silence
I am greeted with smiles,
And congratulations,
And tears
That mean
Someone was touched
By my words?

Why is that?

All of us feel lonely at times. No one is immune. Sometimes that loneliness is just from fatigue. We are tired, and want someone there to console us. And even when we know it is impossible for anyone but God to do that, there can still be an ache and a sorrow that does not go away. This is from feeling like that once.

7-21-1995
A car careens
Across a double yellow
Into my lane.
Today
I don't feel like moving.
Even if the alternative
Is emptiness.
Even if the alternative is nothing.
Even if there is no alternative.

My mind and heart
Go numb.
My hands
Stay straight on the wheel.
"He must not have seen me,"
The other driver will say,
"He didn't even flinch."
But it isn't blindness.
It isn't pain.
It isn't fear
It's loneliness
Here.

At Bible camp, we get to hear lots of stories that counselors and other pastors tell in worship around the campfires a night. Many of these stories are told and retold, but there is often some freshness because they are told by someone who thinks they are something new. And it doesn't hurt to hear again and again, how God loves us. This poem comes from a story about how early Christians would do more than what was expected, to show how much they loved.

7-27-1995

The second mile
Is not measured
In yards,
But in each footstep.
In each drop of sweat.
In each exchanged pleasantry.

Love is not measured
By time,
Or locale,
But with each sorrow overcome.
With each laugh shared.
With each touch.
With each tear.

As one who likes to work out hard, including running, lifting weights, jumping, and push myself when I hike and canoe and kayak, I am in pretty good shape, especially for my age. When I was younger, I used to love to push my body to its limits, and I could. I had a strength that came from something deeper than just the physical. One day at camp, I realized where that strength came from. This was written that day.

7-27-1995
My strength
Comes,
Not from hair or muscle.
Not from any sinuous material.
My strength
Comes
From a dead man
Arisen.
From a God who created,
Suffered,
Forgave,
Out of love.

My strength
Comes
From a source
That makes me dance creatively
Longer than anyone can.
That makes me endure pains
Harder than anyone should.
That makes me love
Deeper than anyone will.

My strength
Comes.

Sometimes it is hard to write sermons. It may be a difficult text. It may have been a difficult week. There may be some pressing issue that needs to be addressed. It may be that I am tired. But it needs to be done, because that is what we do. But sometimes, it seems as if the words do not come. This is from one of those times.

8-3-1995

Words

Do not come easily

Today.

I pull at them

In my mind.

Needing to find

What to say

As I stand in a pulpit

Another Sunday.

Crying tears for those who hurt.

Loving those who till the dirt.

Laughing at children who flirt.

And I pray

And listen to music

As it lays its crescendos

Down.

But I frown.

Because those words

Lie still.

At times, pastors doubt, and wonder, and cry to God like everyone else. We are not immune to doubt and sin. And, like everyone else, it usually comes when we are tired and overworked. When we want some special thing to come and deliver us. Of course, God doesn't usually work that way. Usually God asks us to work, and love, and think a little bit. This came on one of those days when I wanted God to come and make things better, and God didn't. At least, not the way I wanted. And it reminded me of other times when I wanted this too.

11-29-1995
I cry to God
For a sign.
A shooting star.
A whisper from the wind.
A friend's special word.
But
All I have
Are these tears.
These memories.
These empty,
Dull,
Moments.
Times
Spent walking,
Lumbering,
In the house.
Leaning on a wall.
Looking out a window.
Crying all the time.
I can only remember
The good.
I can only cry
Over what has been lost.
I can only
Ask
For a sign.

I have always tried to write a poem for my Christmas cards. I haven't been as successful as I would like, but I often think about what Christmas means each year, and at the least, write one for myself. It is a poignant time, and as the years pass, a time to look at the joys and the sorrows that people feel. One year, I realized that Christmas is simply God keeping a promise. The promise to deliver us. This is from that year.

12-12-1995
An old couple,
Who hold hands
And fall fast asleep
After their family
Celebrates
Their 60th anniversary,
Is a promise kept.

A young Abe Lincoln,
Who walks through the snow
With frost nipped ears
To return a penny,
Is a promise kept.

A child,
Who lies crying
In a cold,
Smelly,
Feeding trough,
Yet whose mother coos,
"It's Ok baby."
Is a promise kept.

A man
Who cries in pain
"Why me?"
As he struggles to breathe
On a cross,
Is a promise kept.

There is often a disconnection between pastors and their congregation. For years, it was encouraged. The "Herr Pastor" model was the ideal. The pastor was the expert. He was seen as an aloof and unemotional leader. That's not me. But I know that there is a separation. Just tell people you are a pastor, (even if you aren't) and see the reaction. I wondered about this, and wrote the following as I wondered.

12-14-1995
A pulpit
Serves as a pedestal
Too often.
Instead of intimacy,
There is distance.
Height.
Curiosity.
An altar rail
Can close off
One from another.
A pew
Separates us.
But a baptismal font
Of marble,
Wood,
Even plastic,
Holds us together.
Those drops of water
That seem to evaporate
Are really
Eternal.

Sometimes there are moments, or people, or memories, or other things, that give us energy and keep us going. They may be planned, like vacations and sabbaticals, but usually they aren't. They are often little moments of grace, and they give us joy, so that we can endure what we need to endure, and go on. I honesty can not remember the exact occasion for this poem, but I suspect it was something like that.

12-24-1995
A card
Slipped into my hand
In the receiving line.
A word
Whispered in my ear
As I walk to the sacristy door.
A prayer
Spoken silently
To God.
A joke.
A tear.
A moment of grief.
All things,
Moments I share
That keep me going.
Keep me trying.
Keep me alive
With hope and joy.
A wind
The rustles the trees
And grass
Says to me
"Yes,
Keep going"

One day I was imagining what it would be like to lose a young person in the congregation. Not anyone particular, but someone in general. A few months later, it happened. At the time I wrote this, I did not realize how true it was. Now I do.

1-16-1996
There are no words
Sweet enough
To take away the hurt.
There are no touches
Magical enough
To send sadness
Packing away.
There is only a hole.
Sorrow.
Pain.
An emptiness
That one day
Will be filled,
But for now sits,
Lonely.
Deep.
Hollow.

In early March of 1996, a man walked into a school and shot several children and teachers. No one could understand it. I don't think we ever fully will. And unluckily, it seems to have become more common. This was written afterward, as we all struggled to make some kind of sense out of the senseless.

3-30-1996

A man

Puts a gun in his hand

And walks

Angrily to a school.

Where innocents

And innocence

Play.

Evil grips his heart.

Violence plays it's part,

As children run

Screaming.

Fearing.

Crying.

Dying.

Until only a whimper,

A whisper of the play

Is left.

Maybe God can understand

What would drive a man

To this?

A lot of times during grief, people look back. They try to figure out what they did wrong. What they could have, or should have, done differently. I understand that as a process of grief, and I let them do this as long as they need. Just listening to what they need to say, because they are not ready for anything more. Sometimes this takes a long time. Eventually though, they get to a place where they can look ahead. They must, or else they will not move forward. This time comes, even when people are not ready. This is about that.

4-23-1996
Hollow questions
Of
What could I have done
Or not done
to change the changes.
To prevent the pain.
Hollow,
Because the past is more firm
Than granite.
So,
I ask the real question.
What now?
What do I,
We,
Do?
What do I,
We,
Want?
And though no answer comes
Now,
It will.
And I can not prevent it
No matter how many stones
I use.

One of my personality traits, which often gets in the way of things I want to do, is humor. I know it's an incredibly useful thing. It can break silence. It can loosen people up. It can bring people together. But it can also be seen as insensitive. It can be seen as uncaring. I struggle with this, because it is who I am, and with what I do, people expect sincerity. But it is also hard, because having to deal with grief, sexual abuse, and many others aspects of sin, it is really hard to take some things as seriously as some do. This was written to explain this truth to anyone who wondered.

5-15-1996
Perhaps you wonder,
Why is he telling a joke?
Why is he so goofy?
Why is he laughing
Now?

All I offer,
In defense
Of the indefensible,
Is that
It is hard
To see people die.
Too young.
Too old.
To hear people cry
Over old hurts.
New pains.
To smell the sweat
Of those afraid of dying,
And those working to maintain lives.
To feel the tears
On my sleeves.
It is hard
To experience these things
And take the rest of life
Seriously.

After a long winter, people are ready to move, to get out and do something. It's called cabin fever, after pioneers who spent the winters in their cabins and were ready for spring. It still happens here in the middle of Wisconsin. I think it's part of life. Life doesn't just sit still. There are changes to be made, new beings to create, and new life that must come. This poem came after a long winter, and a time when I was ready to move.

5-28-1996

Spring cries forth

Her wings stiffened

From her night

Of slumber.

But she unfolds

Slowly.

Lumbering,

Like a new born colt.

Opening,

Like a green apple bud.

Spring cries,

And comes,

As she always does.

Because life

Will not

Be held

Back.

A lot of times we are impatient. We want things done right now, or maybe even yesterday. But the real world doesn't work that way, especially when it comes to relationships. And God knows this. God tends to be slow and deliberate. It is one of the reasons why I don't think God created the world in seven normal days. There are lots of other reasons too, but God does everything in a different time frame than ours. It took millions of years to create this world. It took thousands of years for God to send Jesus. It takes us a long time to accept that forgiveness. And for anyone who tries to do things faster, it won't work.

6-1-1996
God created
One dollop at a time.
A word here.
A word there.
And life
Sprang.
Satan came
Trying to have it all at once.
Trying to sear souls
By the millions.
But God,
In his slow,
Slow,
Movements,
Came
Around
Again
To
Save
Us.

I remember this occasion very well. Not the details, but the emotions. I was playing volleyball in a local sand tournament. Someone said something mean to me. I don't remember who or what, but I remember feeling angry and wanting to say something that would hurt them back, but I couldn't think of anything. It bothered me for several days. I finally wrote this, and it probably applies to most of us at one time or another.

6-9-1996

How can a fool
Cause such an impact
In your life?
How can idiots
Raise your ire
To the point
Where you desire
There absence?
How do you take leave
Of the anger you feel
Over infidels
Who cast their spells
Leaving ripples of stupidity
In their wake?

What is true freedom? It's a question many people ask, although not in those terms. How can I retire and not worry? What if the person I love dies? How can I avoid losing my home? How can I get my homework done? And being rich, and healthy, and smart can alleviate some of that. But ultimate freedom comes from outside self. It comes from the realization that you are loved. Not only by those who profess it, but those who show it, including God. True freedom is knowing that you are loved, and letting the rest take care of itself.

6-22-1996
"Freedom,"
Cried the former slave,
As he crossed the river
To the north.

"Freedom,"
Cried the man,
Imprisoned in a concentration camp,
As the Allied soldiers
Carried his emaciated body
Past the barbed wire.

"Freedom,"
Cried the woman,
As her common law husband was sentenced
For his years of abuse.

"Freedom,"
Cried the world,
As the sun blackened,
And the curtain ripped,
And a Centurion watched,
And Mary and the disciples wept,
And the Sanhedrin smiled,
And Christ died.

It's interesting being a pastor. You have to deal with people of all ages and the problems that come with different ages. The issues of young children, parents, teenagers, and the elderly are not the same issues. Not that this is big news. But too often, people don't realize that the issues will change as they age. Older people tend to understand this, as they have lived some of it. But young people too often think things will be the same forever. Hoping that they will be young and strong and in love forever. This poem looks at an imaginary couple who are like that.

6-26-1996
Young boy and girl
Hold hands
In the back of the auditorium.
Concert sounds
Surround them,
But little do they hear
Or see.
They are in love.
But what do they know
At 15.
Will their desire
Be strong enough
To overcome the quarrels,
The rages,
The silence,
That comes as people age?
Will hormones last
Until Alzheimer's and cancer come?
Do they really know
True love?

All of us want God to come directly to us and tell us what he wants. Tell us what to do. Tell us how to live our lives. Unfortunately, God doesn't work that way very often. Usually it is through others, or Scripture, or the Holy Spirit in some fashion. But what would it be like if God did? Here is a possible answer.

7-12-1996

I have spoken to God.

In that brief moment

Between sleep and wake,

God touched me.

I felt the warmth,

That peace,

Come upon me.

I smiled,

Slyly,

And I spoke.

Of course,

"Thank You,"

Was all I could mutter.

But believe me

When I say,

That was just

What God wanted.

Despite the technological advances we have made over the past thousands of years, we are still sinful creatures. We are still driven by greed, selfishness, sin. It seems as if we are trying to make new towers of Babel, and still fail. And it will probably never change. This is about that.

7-12-1996
A craft flies up and out.
To the moon
And beyond.
A submarine explores a cavern
2 miles beneath the waves.
A doctor assembles
A new hip
For an 80 year old woman.
A drug is given
To a child
To prevent tics and seizures.
All these wonderful things,
And yet,
We still
Shoot our family,
Rape our daughters,
Stab our neighbor.

Closer to God
We imagine we climb.
But never
Close enough.

Sometimes, in the middle of worship, I feel love, deep love, for those present. It's not that I don't love them all the time, but there are some times when it seems so clear. As if this is exactly the place we were all meant to be at this time. This was written after one of those times.

7-21-1996
Have you ever
Heard a hymn
Sung so boldly
That your heart leapt?

Have you ever
Cried a tear
In the silence
Of your confession?

Have you ever
Felt true courage
As you began the creed,
"I believe."

Have you ever been
Uplifted?
Challenged?
Touched?
Changed
By the word?

Have you ever?

I was at camp one summer, when I got the news that one of the youth of our congregation had died. There are other poems more specifically about his family and that grief, but on the way home, I had to stop and write. Something. Anything. The truth. This is what came.

7-23-1996
Do you know
How hard it is to drive a car
When there are tears
Streaming
Down your cheeks?

Do you know
How hard it is
To write
When you twitch,
And sigh,
And your body stutters
From the grief?

Do you know
What it's like
To want to just to lay
In fetal position?

Do you know
What it's like
To want to scream at the world,
"Stop!"
But all you can do
Is sit there?

Do you know?

One of the most important lessons a pastor can learn is to shut up. To not talk so much, that it overshadows what is going on. This is especially true in times of grief. People don't need your ideas. People don't need your counsel. People don't need your supposed words of wisdom. They need you. They need you to help them get it out. They need you to listen. I am lucky enough to have learned this early. But it is still hard to do. This was written as I as learning that truth.

7-24-1996
It used to be
That when people cried to me
Of their woes
I would tell them
I was sorry
And that others
Struggled too.
Life was hard.
It used to be
When my friends wondered aloud
About God,
Relationships,
Death,
I would,
At the least,
Give them my opinion.
But
I have learned.
And now,
When people complain,
Question,
Wonder,
I
Remain silent.

One of the most memorable moments in my life was a few days after a horrific tragedy. I had been helping a family grieve the loss of their beloved son, dealing with my own grief, and telling the kids who were at Bible camp about the youth who had died. I was worn out. In the back of my mind I wondered if this was what ministry was going to be. But as I was driving down the road, a flock of doves flew by me in unison, and my heart was lighter. I don't know what it was exactly, but I knew that things would get better for all of us. This was written later that evening.

7-25-1996
The tears have stopped
For now.
I can see
A flock of doves,
Flying up,
And turning right,
In unison.
I can feel
My heart
Begin to move.
I can sense
That one day
Joy
Will come again.

This poem was written just off the cuff, for the fun of it. But a few days after I wrote it, I was talking to one of the counselors at Bible camp who had just returned from Tanzania and was looking for a place to move to, a place to settle down and live her life. I showed her this, and she thought it was very appropriate.

7-25-1996
Home
Is not where your parents live,
Or where your clothes lie,
Or where your key fits.
Home
Is that whisper
In your heart
That says,
"Stay."

I have seen grown men cry, and not be ashamed. They have had good reason. I have seen strong men reduced to nothing, simply because someone they love is in pain. I have been there when men have been crushed, because some part of life has been ruined. And they have all been normal, natural, real. It is a part of who we are, because it is a part of who God is.

8-2-1996
He weeps.
Holding his head
In his hands
As tears
Seep through.
He weeps.
And he is
the father of a dead child.
He is the brilliant businessman
Who has blundered,
Costing his company
Millions.
He is the athlete
Who missed the tape
By milliseconds.
He is the God
Whose son cries,
"Lama sabbacthani!"
Why?

I was working as a volunteer at Bible Camp for a week one summer. I used my vacation so I could work maintenance. I did it because one of my favorite summers was the summer I worked maintenance at a Bible Camp. I got to chain saw. Fix things. Drive the vehicles. And still be in skits and services. One night during the week I volunteered, I walked out of the dining hall, and the sun seemed fixated. It was brilliant yellow and laid a straight line right at whoever looked at it. I thought about it later than night, and this is what came.

8-15-1996
Sunset beams
Dapple the lake
In yellow hues,
Save
For a straight line
Of brilliant white
That will not
Let me go.
Wherever I trod.
Wherever I move.
It points to me.
Warming me.
Annoying me.
Charming me.
I wonder
If God is not the same way.
So large,
So bright,
So brilliant,
Yet
Drawing a straight line
To our hearts
Wherever
We trod.

The idea of love is a strange one. Poets and sages have written thousands of words through the ages, and captured it brilliantly, and not at all. I was thinking about how hearts seem to collect all the refuse there is, and how that affects us. But as I was writing, I also realized that the human heart is not just some finite object, but a vehicle for love. That changed the direction I went.

8-15-1996
The heart
Can be a garbage can.
Collecting whatever refuse
Is given
Until it is so full
It is deemed
Useless.
But a heart
Can also be
A balloon.
Filling with air.
Love.
Joy.
Until it appears there is no room
And an explosion comes.
And you suddenly realize
There's a lot more room
Now
Then you thought.

Sometimes nature herself seems to set the tone. There are days when it is dark, and it seems appropriate. Sometimes nature and your heart seem in sync. They come at good times, and at bad times. I don't remember the exact occasion, but I believe I was remembering a not so good time.

8-22-1996
He walks
Down the sidewalk.
Splashing in puddles.
Watching,
As the trees
Drop the rain
That hadn't made it through
In somber,
Elegant
Tears.
He sniffles.
Remembering another time.
Another rain shower.
Another night
Where his heart
Was much higher
Than now,
As it shuffles along
Just below
His heel.

Being a pastor can be lonely. Even with a supportive spouse and family, people do not always understand. How can they? How can you express the worry and anxiety and sorrow you feel, when you don't always know how or why yourself. Sometimes you just have to sit in silence, and bear it.

9-7-1996
No one to tell
Of this dry well
Swelling
Up inside.
No one to cry
Or share the sigh
Nigh
Upon my breast.
No one to share
My greatest care.
Dare,
I fight my fear?
No,
Rather,
To sit somber,
Sullen,
Sad,
Through
A long dark night
Until the sliver of dawn
Lights the horizon.

H.M. was a man who had battled cancer for a long time. He had a loving family, but an even greater sense of humor. As it neared the end, he just didn't seem to want to let go. His family came and was there for days. Everyone had said goodbye. We had shared prayers, and were ready. But he didn't seem to be ready. Until one day when everyone was around him again. For some reason, he seemed ready, and he was gone a few minutes later. This was written during the difficult time when you know they are not here, but they are also not there.

9-7-1996
You
Have had a gallant fight.
A battle
To be envied
And boasted about.
But it is time now
For rest.
It is best
To grab God's hand
As it extends.
You have lived
With honor
And humor.
With a cackle and openness
That has lifted your burdens
And added more.
But it is time.
Your room is ready.
Your heart must let go
Of the feint whisperings
Of our love
And grasp
True grace.

Most pastors find a way to release the emotional baggage we find ourselves carrying. Some do it with television. Some do it with music. Some do it with friends. I tend to do it with exercise and writing. But, we all need to do it.

9-11-1996
No one knows
The rages.
No one knows
The pages
In the diary.
No one knows
The fiery passion.

No one knows,
Because I choose
To keep it in.
I choose
To keep it
Between God
And myself.
And I don't worry
About who God tells,
Because usually
No one listens.

Sometimes I write things that I make up. I don't know what it is like to lose someone, and be the one who puts on the clothes for their burial. This is what I imagine it to be like.

8-12-1999 The Changing

I slowly unbutton her blouse,
Unzip her pants,
Take off her panties.
Just like I had
For 49 years.
Only this time
Was going to be
The last time.
This time,
Instead of a smile,
A tickle,
And warmth,
There was a cold shell.
It used to hold
Her,
But not anymore.
I know she is away
From the pain,
But I am still gentle
With her shell.
Because it held her so long
And so close
To me.

One of the things pastors do a lot of is praying. Not just on Sundays, but in hospitals, in homes, in our offices, in cars. Often, the most sincere tears are not where we expect them, because the most sincere prayers are those that come from the heart.

8-12-1999
Every Sunday
Thousands of people
Fold their hands
And bow their heads.
But they are not
Praying.
They are just
Saying the words
Until the hour is over.
True prayers
Come from true cares.
They come
As you cry beside the casket
Of a dear friend.
As you hold the hand of your child
As they board the bus
On the first day of school.
As you bow,
Not your head,
But your heart,
To ask in earnest
That God
Would part with some of his grace
On to someone
You love.

I was at seminary for a continuing education week, when I realized how tired I was. I wrote this during a lecture on preaching.

10-26-1999 When my Soul Wearies

When my soul wearies
From her battles
Within and without.
When my hearts cries "Uncle"
From too much faith
And too much doubt.
When I need to rest,
Then I need the best
Care.
The best nurturing.
I need to lie cradled
Under my mother hen's wings.
I need to worship
Until my voice and self sing
Like they were meant to.
I need to find a place
Where my heart and my face
Will mirror
The joy I see.
I need a place
To just be.

I don't know how I got the words "Irish iris" in my head, but they were there one day, and I knew I had to write a poem with them. This happens occasionally. And this is what came.

11-3-1999
From Irish iris I arise
To reach my fingers
Beyond the skies.
To bring forth pasture
From verdant thighs
To hear the earth
Sigh her sighs
And then,
To wipe the tears
From crying eyes
And let them enter
Joy's surprise.

One of the things we all battle is hate. All of us are prejudiced. We can't help it. We feel anger, hate, and even apathy towards certain people, especially those different from us. The key is to realize this, and not let it control us. The key is to stop it early enough, before it is too late.

11-18-1999 Hate

It poisons the soul.
Until her acrid residue
Lies at the bottom,
Resting among the dregs
As they sleep away the pain.
She slips away,
Leaving tears and blame
In her wake.
Leaving fears and shame
You can't seem to shake.
She slips away
To a deeper recess,
Further away from the light,
And further away
From reason.
And if you don't catch her
She will slip
All the way.

One of the most difficult things to deal with is addiction. Whether it is drugs or alcohol or something else, it is hard. Those who suffer from the addiction often are not willing to seek help, and those who live with them think they are helping, when they are really enabling them to keep the person addicted. It is hard to live that way.

3-9-2000
You cannot tell
If it's heaven or hell
When you walk through that door.
You don't know
What's in store
Until it's over
And has become a memory
Best forgotten.
Because if it's a moment of joy,
You know it's only temporary.
And if it is a moment
Of sorrow and sadness,
If it feels like madness,
It lasts too long.

There is a theology that says God controls everything. If someone dies, it is because God wants them for an angel. If someone is hurt, God is testing. If someone gets a better job or wins money, they are being blessed. There is also a theology that says God doesn't care. That he is dead. Somewhere in the middle is the truth.

6-12-2000
Sometimes God
Just watches.
Hoping for us to turn
And catch a glimpse of grace.
Like that girl whose face
You see in the hall
Briefly.
Your eyes meet,
And you share a moment
Of something.

Sometimes God
Just waits.
Ready to share our tears
If we would just
Overcome our fears
And let sorrow escape.
Cascading off
Onto the ground.

Sometimes God
Just aches.
Seeing our mistakes
And wondering why
We don't come to him,
But cry
And sigh,
And die,
In anguish.

I like to use nature to describe how we think. Flowers, clouds, trees, seeds are all natural things that can be used as metaphors for us. It works well because people know those things. I think that might be one reason Jesus did it.

6-16-2000
Gray clouds sit,
Somber,
Still.
Almost as if
They had a will
Of their own.
But a soft wind blows
And shows
Who really
Has the power.

The following is a benediction I wrote.

6-16-2001
May the love of God attend you,
The grace of God defend you,
The mercy of God suspend you
From pain and sorrow
Today and tomorrow and tomorrow.

There have been three times when I have seen the moon sitting huge in the sky, looking almost close enough to touch. And every time it happens, I write about it. This was the last time.

8-8-2001
Who saw that moon
Last night?

Whose eyes beheld the sight
Of silver clouds that broke away
To let the light of day
From the other side of the world
Fall upon us?
Whose heart
Could not sit still,
But sat gazing out
The window sill
In hope?
Whose soul shared,
What God had bared
To all the world,
That even darkness
Can not hold back
Light.

Who saw that moon
Last night?

When I remarried, I promised my wife I would write her a poem for lunch every day she was working. Luckily she is a teacher and works 180 days. I have done more, but here are some.

8-25-2000 #5

Of all the shadows
That cover the world,
None is darker
Than the black solitude
Of loneliness.

Of all the light
That chases shadows away,
None is brighter
Than spending a day
With you.

9-17-2000 #19

What does love feel like?
Is it the same thing
As riding your bike down a long hill
While the wind whips your hair?
Or is it laughter
As you see your neighbor take a spill
On an icy sidewalk?
Or could it be peace
From the release of tension
After people have waited
And watched?
No,

continued

Love feels like your skin
Next to mine.
Warm.
Soft.
There.

10-22-2000 #40
Where thou art,
There will my heart
Reside.
No longer willing to hide
What I feel
From the rest of the world.
But letting my love
Fly unfurled
Until the wind dies
To a whisper.

12-4-2000 #68
The Word made flesh
Appeared
2,000 years ago,
But grace
Had not touched me
Until I saw you so.
Just standing.
Your daughter and you
As a western wind blew
And then I knew.
I knew.
I knew.
I knew,
Love was incarnate.

I had a period where I wrote several pieces about God. I don't know why I had the urge to do this, or why I did it, but it sometimes happens like this. These are some of what came during that period.

11-7-2001
Why
Was Jesus born
In some forlorn,
Forgotten
Place?
With the first face to see
A young mother still sweating
From the pain?
And why did he grow up
A carpenter's son?
And why did he die
A painful death
On the cross?

He was born
So that he could know
What it was
To live and breathe and die.

He was a carpenter's son,
So that while his hands grew calloused,
His heart would not.

He died in pain
So joy could fall
Like spring rain
Upon us.

11-14-2001
You
Are shade in the desert
And covering in a storm.
Whatever the hurting need
To keep them safe and warm.
Yet,
You also call for justice,
Righteousness
And peace.
For my life to turn upside down,
And conflict to increase,
While I proclaim your word.
You
Are too far beyond measure.
Too far to simply treasure
And leave buried in a hole.
You
simply are
The being who cares
Enough
To allow death
And to overcome it.

D.O. lost his wife to a heart attack, and as we were talking after the funeral, he was telling me about how lonely and less life seemed, even though he was busy with his kids and other things. I didn't say much. I couldn't. But I listened, and then wrote this.

6-27-2002
Life is not empty.
There is still job,
Children,
Friends.
But when the joy
In your life
Meets her end
It is different.
I guess,
When you have tasted
The ultimate tenderness,
And it is gone,
Life is different.

God's testing is not fun. It reminds me of an inoculation. We get the pain, a small amount of the disease, so we will be stronger.

7-23-2002
Sometimes God protects
With pain.
By letting us cry
Our refrain of tears
Until we learn
God's love
Is not an umbrella from the rain.
Rather,
Like a doctor's shot,
We feel a prick,
And no longer are sick
Because our illness
Has been slain.

Grace is a funny thing. God doesn't come and overpower us, or make a big show, or even make it obvious that we are loved. OK, maybe a resurrection is kind of showy, but not so much to us, as we weren't there. God just seems to love us in a slow, quiet way. But God does love us.

7-24-2002
God's love
Does not overpower us
With force.
It is like a river
That makes its course
Through years
Of slowly washing away the soil.
It takes our tears,
And our toil
Into itself,
And cries and sighs
And works alongside us,
Until we see
That truly
God loves us.

As I have engaged in the church wide issues that have come up over the years, I have realized that dialogue and discussion are good. They are necessary. They are the only thing that can conquer the division and hate that we suffer from. It isn't easy, but so important that we start to talk, so we can better understand each other and may, just maybe, learn to get long.

10-22-2002
It is not monologue or debate
That makes hate dissipate
As we talk.
It is dialogue.
Discussion.
Listening to the percussion
Of lips and hearts
That helps us to create
Understanding,
And make even deeper,
Our love.

One of the great tragedies of our time, and really, it has been going on a long time, is the Middle East conflict. A friend of mine visited there, and then she spoke to groups about it. I wondered why the hate is so great, and wrote this.

12-19-2002
Why do so many
Deform our world
When they want to inform the world
Of their pain?
Why this sick refrain of violence
Upon the innocent?
Is the pain so great
That it would negate
The rest of humanity?
What brings this insanity
Of suicide bombers,
Genocide tractors,
And all the other factors
That try to carve out power
From death?

There are all kinds of signs of resurrection and life. Even in the midst of pain, suffering and death, there are stories. This was written in winter, just before Christmas, which can be a busy, almost crazy time.

12-19-2002
A crocus dies
In winter snow.
There is no hocus pocus
To resurrect it,
We must simply let it go.
And wait.
And wonder.
Until spring,
When a bud begins to grow
And we know
Life
Will go on.

A pastor colleague of mine asked me to write a poem for her congregation based on their name, "Emmanuel". This is what came.

2-6-2003
In my tears
I cry the refrain,
"Why won't God
Stop my pain?"
If God is so powerful,
So loving,
So true,
Why does he put us through
Hell?
And then I remember his name.
Emmanuel.
God with us.
In joy and in sorrow.
Sharing all.
Today and tomorrow.
Not taking away,
But adding to life.
Whether it's our laughter
Or our strife.
God will not
Choose his power over love.
He will simply
Be
With us.
In the pain,
The rain,
The insane moments
That make life
What it is.

As I have been a pastor, I have written more and more about the church, leadership, and God. It just seems to be what I end up thinking about, partly because of job, and partly because of passion.

5-8-2003
We are a people
Of promise.
Of purpose.
Told that we're loved.
Asked to proclaim.
To turn discord
Into discourse,
By the same force
That died on a tree
To set us free,
And now holds us together
With the thin tether
Of love.

When I think about church leadership, I like to look to the Bible. To those people who led God's people in the Bible, and how they lived. Usually they are not that much different than us.

11-14-2003
For much of his life
Moses wandered in the desert.
When he was young,
It was to escape death
At the hands of his stepfather,
Or so it seemed.
But the real purpose
Was so he could know how to survive.
How to help keep alive
That tattered band
That wandered with him
Those 40 long years.

The longer I am a pastor, the more I realize the depths of sin. How much we hurt each other, and God, through our misdeeds. The cross was not the last time God suffered. God suffers all the time, because of us. And even though we know God loves us, it still hurts him when we do those sinful things we do.

4-9-2004
Every day,
God suffers and dies,
With every death
That comes upon the world.
Every day
God groans and sighs
As another heart
Is broken and unfurled.
Every day
God dies again
As we nail him to the cross
With our actions and our words
Every day.
Every day.

4-19-2004
God's suffering
Did not end on the cross.
It still comes
With every loss we feel.
Every heart we steal.
Every time we deal
In our attempts for gain.
God still cries.
And it comes like rain.
Falling in large somber tears

That can not be held back,
But only fall down
And soak into the ground
Where his blood
Once lay.

Hospital visits can be incredibly intimate and holy times. It is a sacred time when people open up and you share the fears and doubts people have in their pain. I do not know the particular occasion for this poem, but it could have been many.

10-26-2004
It was a sacred moment
As we held hands.
She weakly clung,
As I moved her hospital band.
We said our prayers
And then said our goodbyes,
Knowing,
Through the sharing of touch
And our poignant sighs,
The holy
Was touched again.

Not only do pastors deal with sin and its consequences, we deal with grace. We don't control it, but we do have many opportunities to see it in action. These are about times of grace.

5-6-2005
Grace,
True grace,
Abandons conventions
And shatters the rules.
It reminds us
That we are all fools
Who try to exclude
On belief and race.
But even prejudice
Is in God's embrace.
Because once your heart is stilled
You will find heaven filled
With people,
Who are simply thrilled
To be there.

5-6-2005
God's mercy surprises
Like soft orange sunrises
After a previous storm.
Like expecting a cold bed
And finding it warm.
Only grace
Is even deeper,
Because the price paid
Was steeper
Than we
Can ever know.

The town doctor was dying of cancer. He was not a member, but a friend. I visited him at home while his family was there and we talked about the arrangements. This was written when I got home. I gave a copy to the widow.

2-20-2005
My heart
Goes out to them
As they love him
To death.
As he struggles
With every breath
To speak
What they already know.
That he has loved them
So much
That his heart can not contain it
Any longer
And he must leave
And find
A stronger place
Where love can live
Forever.

For a while I started to write a series on the books of the Bible. So far I have only done a few. Here are the first two.

2-20-2005 Genesis
Out of chaos came a word.
Life was beckoned.
Life was stirred
Into being.
Into seeing.
Into agreeing to continue.
To begin with root and grow to sinew.
In the beginning
Life
Unfurled.
And it started on this world,
Not with shouts.
Not with song.
But with a word
That moved along.

2-20-2005 Exodus
A thousand years
Of silent pain
Cry from the sands
Their sad refrain.
A people who wandered
For forty years.
Had hearts broken,
And spilled their tears.
They cursed God.
And God cursed back.
And in his love
God would lack them
Only one thing.
To hear the trees
Of Canaan sing
While the eastern winds blew
And they knew
They were home.

Two men died and left their wives as widows. As I did the funerals and talked with the women, I thought about how difficult it was to be a widow, or widower, for that matter. I thought about what I would miss, and this is what came.

2-27-2005
I miss being called
Mr. and Mrs.
I miss the surprise
Of his soft kisses
Upon the nape of my neck.
And nothing is so hollow
As the emptiness
Of sleeping alone.
He is gone now,
And my heart aches,
And my lips quake
And quiver,
Every once in a while
When I feel the shiver
Of his soul
Still touching mine.
But
It isn't the same.
And there is no shame
In admitting
What I miss most of all
Is someone to lay with me.
Someone to play with me.
Someone to say with me,
Back and forth,
And back and forth,
"I love you, dear."

G.P. and his wife drove truck together. One day they were at a truck stop and he went in to check some papers. When he got back, she was dead. We talked about it, and he spoke of the pain, the emptiness, the hole in his heart. This was written after that.

5-14-2006
They shared
Over a million miles
In the truck.
Over countless smiles
As they were stuck
In the same cab.
They talked.
They shared.
They loved.
They dared to go as deep into one another
As two can go.
Until her heart stopped.
His seemed to.
Because after years of sleeping
On 50 inches of foam,
He doesn't know
How to be alone.
And so he wanders,
Looking to fill a void.
A hole.
Because her soul
Has left her body,
And he
Was left behind.

I don't remember the occasion, but according to my notes, I saw an old woman at a nursing home with her head down, not knowing if she was even alive. No one checked on her. No one even seemed to care. But this was written after.

12-19-2006
She sat there.
Head bowed down.
In a wheelchair.
In a hall.
No one noticed.
No one cared.
No one
Cared at all
Whether she was alive
Or dead.
They simply walked by,
As she dropped her head,
And her heart,
From the loneliness
Of no one
Noticing
Her pain.

M.J. was an old, wise farmer. He had an incredible amount of common sense, humility, and humor. He didn't like too much attention, but was simply content to know that his crops were doing well, the cows were fine, and the family and friends he loved were doing well too. This was written after he died.

1-16-2007
He was wise.
He was common.
He was plain.
And he would have been proud
To hear himself called that
Again and again.
Because he knew how seed began.
Falling from the farmer's hand.
Slipping into earth's dark soil.
To begin her life long toil.
Reaching for the sun and sky.
Blossoming.
Only to die
And leave
More seeds
For their journey.

S.M. committed suicide at his place of work. He left behind a wife, three kids, parents and siblings. No one knows why this happens. Too often, like this case, we are completely baffled because there weren't clues. In speaking to his wife, she simply talked about the pain, the confusion, the dark cloud that always comes with this kind of loss.

3-26-2007

Emptiness
Is all I breathe in.
Sorrow's darkness
Covers my skin
Like a dark brown dress
That matches
Everything I wear.
That follows me
When I dare
Step outside.
Why can't I hide?
Why can't I
Ignore my pride?
Tell the world
Of his suicide
And how I cried,
And fainted,
And faltered?
Why does it hurt
So deep
And so strong?
When will I be able
To move along?
Not function.
Not live.
But move
From this dark corner?

When my daughter was at Vacation Bible School at a different congregation, she had a wonderful counselor whom she adored. When we went to Bible Camp that summer, I got to know that counselor, and she was wonderful. I told her about how much my daughter, and others, enjoyed her. She was very humble. She thought I was gushing too much. It reminded me of many others who are humble and loving. I wrote this and gave her a copy.

6-26-2007
How little you know
Of the hero you are.
Sharing faith,
Like a brilliant white star,
To children who follow
What you do
And who you are.
And maybe
That is best.
So we will not puff our chest,
And put on airs,
But continue to love.
Continue to care.
Because we do not know
The love we show
As we simply
Live our lives
In joy.

One winter I decided to have fun days. Once a month we would gather at our Parish Hall and simply have fun. Sometimes it was Uno or Pictionary. Sometimes it was movies. It was just a time to gather and get closer by having fun. They were successful, because that is exactly what we did.

11-30-2007
You don't need to be
A human dictionary
To play the game
Of Pictionary.
You can even draw the worst pictures
Of porcupines
And buffalo.
All that matters
Is that you go,
And laugh,
And love,
And know,
That you are
Building community.

S.M. lost her husband to suicide. He had suffered from depression for years. He was on medication, but it got to be too much, and so one day he hung himself in their garage. She discovered him. A week after the funeral she was standing in the graveyard as I was leaving after worship. This was written when I got home.

4-2-2007
There she stood,
Solitary figure by the grave.
Wondering why she couldn't save
Him.
She stood,
For a long, long time.
Thinking of him
And their sublime
Moments.
She shares her heart,
Which is darker
Than the black coat she wears,
And she tells him
Of the rips and tears
He still gives.
Eventually,
After her cries and sighs,
She whispers to him
Her tender goodbyes,
And she hopes
She is leaving him in the ground.
But
She knows better.

About the Author

Mike Vetsch has been writing poetry for over 30 years, and has been the pastor of a rural Wisconsin church for the past 19 years. He lives in Nelson, Wisconsin with his wife and daughter.

CPSIA information can be obtained at www.ICGtesting.com
Printed in the USA
LVOW11s0440050813

346055LV00004BB/11/P